British Heritage Series

LANDSCAPES *of* ENGLAND

Published in Great Britain 1985 by Crown Books.
CLB 1377
Crown Books is a registered imprint of Colour Library Books Ltd.,
© 1985 Illustrations and text: Colour Library Books Ltd.,
   Guildford, Surrey, England.
Display and text filmsetting by Acesetters Ltd.,
   Richmond, Surrey, England.
Produced by AGSA, in Barcelona, Spain.
Printed and bound in Barcelona, Spain by Rieusset and Eurobinder.
All rights reserved.
ISBN 0 86283 334 5
DEP. LEGAL 14.887

British Heritage Series

LANDSCAPES of ENGLAND

CROWN BOOKS

So much has been written about England; there is no other country which has been so eulogised throughout the centuries; and so much has been written of the fierce pride that dwells within the English breast.

It is not surprising that this tiny country reveals such a rich diversity of landscape, for although comparatively young on the geological time scale, its complex structure, spanning 600,000,000 years, illustrates a surprising range of geological history, from the oldest igneous rocks of the extreme west and north to the recent alluvial soils of reclaimed fenland in East Anglia. By the time the North Sea had been formed (about 6,000 B.C.) and the mainland link with France severed, the island was populated by hunters who were also to become skilled in the arts of carpentry and fishing, and who were later joined by foreign immigrants, including a short, swarthy-complexioned Mediterranean people who settled in the Cotswolds and on the chalk hills, about 2,400 B.C. These New Stone Age farmers, the first in Britain, were responsible for the building of the long, narrow burial mounds, or barrows, predominantly conspicuous on the chalk downlands, and the megalithic tombs that were built by the settlers along the western coast.

By the end of the New Stone Age, Britain's most famous and awe-inspiring megalithic monument – Stonehenge – was under construction, with the completion of the outer circular ditch and bank, a ring of 56 pits known as the Aubrey Holes just inside the bank, and the Heel Stone which stands 256 feet from the centre circle on the avenue leading from the northeastern break in the bank. During the second millennium, about 1,800 B.C., the Beaker Folk appeared on this island, their arrival coinciding with the dawn of the Bronze Age. They played a major role, not only in the second stage of development at Stonehenge with the transportation of the pillars of igneous rock or 'bluestones' from the Prescelly Hills in South-West Wales, but also in the creation of the fascinating Avebury Stone Circles – some one hundred sarsen stones of huge dimensions – which ring the picturesque Wiltshire Village. Stonehenge was later remodelled during the 15th century B.C. when about eighty huge blocks of sarsen were brought from the Marlborough Downs to form a unique circle, with its carefully shaped lintels and trilithons, and inner horseshoe formation, the remains of which can still be seen today.

From the brooding mystery of Stonehenge to the northern limit of Roman occupation – Hadrian's Wall – England has a wealth of fascinating history which is woven into the very fabric of its hills and dales, bustling towns and cities, sleepy villages and sea-washed shores and, in spite of the fact that over the centuries the landscape has been significantly changed by its occupants, the basic structure of life in scattered groups, whether in modern cities or close-knit villages, perpetuates the picture of England as a pastoral country that still persists even in the 20th century.

Until modern times Cornwall was virtually isolated from the rest of the country, the Tamar River forming a formidable barrier with neighbouring Devon as it slices across the peninsula from Woolley Barrow to the Plymouth Sound, until Brunel's elegant Victorian bridge at Saltash carried the railway across the river. This feeling of remoteness is nowhere better illustrated than in the lonely Longships Lighthouse, standing beyond the granite grandeur of Land's End, at the tip of the Penwith Peninsula, where countless ships have perished on the merciless rocks.

From The Lizard, the southernmost part of England, with its soaring cliffs and pinnacles of rock reaching down to Lizard Point, up to Camborne, once the centre of Cornwall's tin mining industry, and beyond, the old pump houses, once so necessary to the miners to guard against the flooding with which they were constantly threatened, still dot the landscape. Cliff-top churches perch above the craggy bluffs that overlook the sand and shingle beaches; cob and thatched cottages line the winding country lanes of Devon amid the rich, red-soiled farming land, and slate and granite cots hug the inland, windswept moors. Stirring reminders of past history, such as Pendennis Castle at Falmouth; Restormel Castle, close to Lostwithiel; the Methodist 'Cathedral' at Gwennap Pit, where John Wesley preached in the mid-18th century, and St Michael's Mount, opposite Penzance, which, according to legend, is part of the lost kingdom of Lyonnesse, where King Arthur's knights once rode, kindle the imagination, while the bleak and wild moors of Bodmin and Dartmoor are renowned for their rugged, isolated beauty.

Cornwall's cathedral city and administrative centre is Truro, noted for its striking, triple-tiered cathedral which was completed in 1910. For eight centuries the Sees of Cornwall and Devon were united, until the reconstitution of the Cornish See in 1897.

Exeter, in Devon, the South West's major city, and one of England's most historic, contains the remains of one of the largest Roman bath houses ever to be excavated in Britain, as well as a magnificent 14th-century cathedral noted for its two outstanding Norman towers and renowned carved figures on the West Front; plus a wealth of fine buildings, mansions, castles and abbeys.

It was from Plymouth, the largest city in the West Country, that the Pilgrim Fathers, aboard the *Mayflower*, set sail for America in 1620. Here, over three centuries later, in 1966, the city witnessed the start of another epic journey, that of Sir Francis Chichester, as he commenced his successful single-handed voyage around the world.

One of the South West's showpieces is undoubtedly picturesque Clovelly, lying in a lush, narrow combe between the steep Devon cliffs. Cars are banned from the village and the precipitous main street is almost continually filled with fragrant, colourful flowers. East of sophisticated Torquay, Devon's largest and most famous seaside resort, is the spectacular Kent's Cavern, occupied by prehistoric men and animals during the last Ice Age, and one of the oldest known human dwelling-places in Britain.

Surrounded by myth and legend, Glastonbury in Somerset, lying on slopes that incline from the Brue Valley to a 522-ft tor, topped by the fragmented remains of the Benedictine abbey of St Mary, is the cradle of Christianity in Britain. It is said that when Joseph of Arimathea came to the town, bringing with him the chalice used at the Last Supper, he leant in prayer on his thorn staff, which immediately took root, indicating that he should stay and found a religious house. The winter-flowering Glastonbury thorn-tree that sprang from the original root on Wirrall Hill is purported to have been hacked down by a Roundhead during the Civil War, but a thorn-tree in the abbey grounds is claimed to be a cutting from it. According to the monks of Glastonbury, King Arthur, whose Camelot is thought by some to be Cadbury Castle, near Sutton Mentis, and his Queen, Guinevere, were reinterred in the abbey, and the Holy Grail, brought by Joseph, and which Arthur's knights sought, is believed to be buried below the Chalice Spring on Glastonbury Tor.

Considered to be the loveliest part of Somerset, the undulating, wooded Quantock Hills have close affinities with the poets Coleridge and Wordsworth, who strolled amid the dark, tangled woods and heather-covered moorland, whilst the lonely Mendip Hills are rent by the towering limestone cliffs of the awe-inspiring Cheddar Gorge.

Facing the Severn estuary and the southern part of the Cotswolds Hills, the county of Avon contains the spectacular Avon Gorge, spanned by Brunel's remarkable Clifton Suspension Bridge towering 245 ft above the Avon River's high-water level and affording some of the finest panoramic views of the gorge and surrounding countryside. Bristol, combining old and new in pleasing proportions, has been a thriving commercial port since the 10th century. It was from this important city that John Cabot set sail in search of North America and Newfoundland, in 1497, in the 100-ton *Matthew*, and in 1552 was founded the Society of Merchant Venturers, who played such an important role in the development of the mighty Empire.

Around the Roman baths of the settlement of Aquae Sulis, chosen for the valuable mineral waters that originate in the Eastern Mendips, grew the beautiful city that was to take their name and which was to come to the full flowering of its grace and charm during Georgian times. Although prosperous throughout the Middle Ages, Bath's fame is closely associated with the high society of the Regency period, when the talented dandy, Beau Nash, presided over the pump-room balls and elegant assemblies, so delightfully described in Jane Austen's 19th-century novels.

As famous as the prehistoric monuments that rise from the vast stillness of Wiltshire's Salisbury Plain, New Sarum, or Salisbury, built at the confluence of four river valleys, and one of the loveliest of England's many cathedral cities, is famed for its magnificent centrepiece, set amid a splendid conglomeration of varying architectural styles: the resplendent mediaeval cathedral with its majestic, soaring spire and graceful cloisters, eulogised by Trollope. Among its many treasures is one of the four original copies of the Magna Carta, now housed in the library over the East Walk. West of the city lie the valleys of the Wylye and the Nadder, divided by the forest downlands of Grovely Wood and the Great Ridge, along which can be traced the route of a Roman road as it swings west towards Bath.

Dorset is rich farming country, famous for its rolling pastures

providing its creamy milk and delicious cheeses. Immortalised by the great English novelist and observer of rural life, Thomas Hardy, who was born in the picturesque hamlet of Bockhampton, the pastoral scenes provide memorable backgrounds to many of his famous novels. Belying the undisturbed, rural tranquillity, however, is a dramatic coastline, particularly impressive in the crumbling, limestone cliffs which culminate in Durdle Door, a massive natural arch of Purbeck stone that guards the entrance to Man O' War Bay.

England, as a maritime nation, has always had strong associations with the sea. Nowhere is this more evident than along the coast of Hampshire. Buckler's Hard may seem an unlikely setting today, with horses grazing on the wide, main street, but it was here, in the 18th century, that many of the ships were built which were to sail under the command of Nelson in the Napoleonic Wars. This naval tradition is carried out, and brought up to date, at Portsmouth, with its great dockyards and training schools, and a poignant reminder of its past is Nelson's flagship, the *Victory*, berthed among sheds of red brick and concrete in the dockyard itself, on board which this most famous of England's naval heroes died.

Synonymous with Hampshire is the New Forest – the famed royal hunting ground which was a favourite of King John – its vast woodland teeming with a variety of wildlife including the celebrated New Forest pony. Today this oldest of the great forests of England, covering 145 square miles, is administered by a special group of officials, called Verderers, who are responsible for maintaining law and order, in addition to the welfare of the many animals which inhabit the preserve.

Separated from the Hampshire coastline, with its wealth of fine resorts, by the Solent and Spithead, lies the delightful holiday island of the Isle of Wight, a favourite of the Victorians since Queen Victoria endorsed its qualities. It was in the royal country retreat of Osbourne House, in East Cowes, that Queen Victoria died in 1901.

The South Downs are full of natural beauty, and wooded hills and valleys, delightful villages and fine coastal resorts are part of the area's enormous variety. In Sussex, the picturesque old town of Rye, once a lively port, but now left stranded by the receding sea, still retains the character it had when it was a notorious haunt of smugglers. Eastbourne, at one time a small fishing village, is still the elegant resort that the 7th Duke of Devonshire designed in 1834, and nearby Beachy Head, the highest cliff on the south coast, towering 534 ft above the sea, still attracts countless visitors who can, on a clear day, glimpse the Isle of Wight to the west and Dungeness to the east. Brighton, possibly the best-known resort on the Sussex coast, with its fairy-tale Royal Pavilion, is an intriguing confection of graceful Georgian houses, gaudy seaside paraphernalia, bracing sea-air and delightful old shops and houses that line the narrow, picturesque 'Lanes'. Just west of the cathedral town of Chichester lies one of the major Roman relics in Britain, Fishbourne, where excavations have revealed an important Roman palace occupied during the 2nd and 3rd centuries A.D., while southeast of the Black Down, the highest point in Sussex, stands the mediaeval town of Petworth and the magnificent mansion of Petworth House, with its superb art collection that includes a series of exquisite Turner paintings of the local landscapes that the artist loved so well.

Although to many people Surrey conjures up the image of one vast London commuter land, the county has nevertheless managed to retain much of its natural beauty in generous open spaces, such as Box Hill, one of the South East's best known beauty spots on the North Downs and a popular picnic area as long ago as the reign of Charles II, and in its charming villages, rich in historic interest. The very banks of the River Thames, as it winds its way through the countryside, endorse the fact. Runnymede saw the granting by King John of the draft of Magna Carta in 1215 and the site now stands in National Trust Property. Historic Richmond, so named by Henry VII to commemorate his original title of Duke of Richmond, stands on the slopes of a hill from the top of which may be seen a famous and most beautiful view of the river. Nearby Kingston-upon-Thames has been a royal borough for over 1,100 years. Outside the Guildhall may be seen the 'King's Stone' on which several Saxon Kings were crowned. The county also contains some of the country's finest botanical gardens: Kew Gardens

which were landscaped by 'Capability' Brown, and contain the great Palm House and the whimsical Pagoda; the Royal Horticultural Society's delightful 300-acre experimental gardens at Wisley, and Winkworth Arboretum's superb woodland area.

Often referred to as 'the garden of England', Kent has supported orchards and vineyards since Roman times. Hops, too, have been grown in the county for over four thousand years and today the hop fields cover some 10,000 acres, mainly in the Medway Valley and in a belt from Faversham to Canterbury, where traditional, conical-roofed oast houses for hop drying are a familiar and pretty part of the rural scene. Beyond the rich valleys the North Downs stretch towards the Kent coastline, peppered with coastal ports that once presented the first line of defence against invaders, culminating in the famed white cliffs of Dover as they preside over the narrowest part of the English Channel. For centuries Dover has played a major role in British history, and the road, from this busiest of English passenger ports, to Canterbury – the centre of Christianity in England since Saxon times – still follows the route of the Roman Watling Street. To this city mediaeval pilgrims trudged the ancient trackway of the 'Pilgrims Way', so eloquently represented by Chaucer, that they might worship at the shrine of the murdered Thomas á Becket in the long, grey cathedral that dominates the city, and is still the home of the Mother Church of Anglicans throughout the world.

How to describe the truly magnificent city of London, that can be almost all things to all men, and about which countless words have already been written? Ever growing, its very size can be daunting – its contemporary boundaries encompassing a collection of villages, hamlets and even 'new towns' which have, in comparatively recent times, been swallowed up to become part of the vast conglomeration of Greater London. Called by the Romans *Londinium* and defined by city walls that still contain the city proper, it has been added to throughout the centuries to leave a legacy of fine buildings, streets and squares that fan out from the mighty Thames – the broad river to which the city owes much of its importance.

Architectural gems of the past – St Paul's Cathedral, the Tower, Westminster Abbey – the list is endless – all jostle for space amid the newer additions; for example the gleaming high-rise buildings and now-familiar landmark of the Post Office Tower. Yet, as though to balance this wealth of stone, London contains an abundance of parks, gardens and open spaces – the 'green fields of London' – in which to walk along fragrant pathways, or sit beside tranquil lakes, is to forget that sometimes only yards away the silence is broken by the noisy hum of a mighty city hurrying by. All the best to be offered in any city throughout the world can be found here – art galleries and museums, churches and mansions, internationally-known stores and restaurants, and, of course, the country's unique pomp and pageantry that is symbolic of a monarchy which has stood at the nation's helm for over a thousand years.

From its source in the Cotswolds the orderly Thames flows through Oxfordshire and Berkshire, its lush water meadows marking the counties' boundaries. To the south of the river, on the bold escarpment of the Berkshire Downs bordering the fertile, flat farmlands, looms the 374-ft figure of the Uffington White Horse, after which the Vale is named. Myth and controversy surround this gigantic form which, some claim, was cut into the chalk in Saxon times, while others assert that the art-style is similar to that of the Iron Age Celts and believe that the figure is representative of their goddess Epona, protectress of horses. The ancient tracks of the Icknield Way and Ridge Way, as they cross the lovely Berkshire Downs, also give some indication of how far back in antiquity people have occupied the area. Although the county is punctuated with a wealth of historic mansions, the most celebrated is undoubtedly that of Windsor Castle as it dominates the leafy banks of the glorious Thames. Built by William the Conqueror, and improved and embellished by succeeding monarchs, the castle first became a royal home during the reign of Henry I. Contained within its soft grey walls is some of the finest architecture in England, notably in the magnificent St George's Chapel.

Where the Thames meets the Cherwell, in the Upper Thames Basin, and is known as the Isis, rise the honey-coloured stone buildings and 'dreaming spires' of Oxfordshire's crowning glory and its ancient seat of learning – Oxford – part of England's cultural heritage. It was during the 8th century that the city was formed with the founding of St Frideswide's nunnery. By 1214 a university was established and before the close of the 13th century the four colleges of Balliol, Merton, St Edmund Hall and University had been instituted. Over the succeeding centuries other historic colleges swelled their ranks, to where those with propensity would seek the dissemination of knowledge, within those hallowed walls.

Dramatically rent by the low chalk ridge of the Chilterns, the face of Buckinghamshire presents one of England's richest agricultural regions, Creslow Great Field, on its northern profile, and a countryside of beechwoods and bluebells, mossy banks and silver streams on its southern. It was in this county, so full of history, in an old stone church surmounted by a huge, gilded ball, which perches on a hilltop in West Wycombe Park, that the members of the notorious Hell Fire Club, an 18th-century group of gamblers and rakes, met to plot their witchcraft orgies. At Jordan, near Beaconsfield, can be seen beams that formed part of the Pilgrim Fathers' *Mayflower*. Penn was the home of William Penn, the founder of Pennsylvania in the 'New World', and in Chalfont St Giles stands the mellow cottage which was inhabited by Milton when he fled to escape the Great Plague of 1665. Oddly enough, Buckingham is not the county seat, although it once was. It was given the title by Alfred the Great, but lost it in 1725, when the honour was transferred to Aylesbury. The county of Buckinghamshire reflects so admirably the fascination of English history in that it is made up of so many small incidents, as well as the great and the obvious.

From Buckinghamshire the Great Ouse curves its way through the green pasturelands of north Bedfordshire, a peaceful region that has remained unspoilt by the passage of time. Straddling the great river is the county town of Bedford, with its attractive conglomerate of varying architectural styles, closely associated with John Bunyan – of *The Pilgrim's Progress* fame – who spent over half his life in the town (although a great deal of it in Bedford Jail!). This beautiful county displays its most varied scenery in its southernmost tip, where the windblown Dunstable Downs, affording views over nine counties, provide an ideal launching ground for gliders. High on the Downs is sited the internationally-known zoo of Whipsnade, where visitors do not even need to step out of their cars to see many of the animals. Here, too, is the magnificent stately home of Woburn, with its famous Wildlife Park.

Picturesque Hertfordshire, although bisected by arterial roads since Roman times, is one of the country's prettiest counties. Leafy lanes wind and loop through the grassy hills and steep little valleys of the rural countryside, where half-timbered houses and thatched-roofed cottages huddle in numerous scattered villages. Hertfordshire, too, has its rich share of history. The city of St Albans dates back 2,000 years, and is the third important town on the site. Its magnificent abbey, originally built by the Saxons to commemorate Britain's first Christian martyr, St Alban, was rebuilt by the Normans and enlarged in the 13th century. West of the city stands the splendid, ruined remains of Verulamium, one of the finest Roman towns in England, exhibiting a fine example of a huge theatre which dates from the mid-2nd century A.D., in addition to important remains that are housed in a nearby museum.

Essex is a county of immense contrasts, from the great forested acres of Epping that border the sprawling metropolis of Greater London, through the bustle of industry of the Thames-side area where the bright lights of Southend-on-Sea beckon Londoners to their favourite seaside resort, to the coastal belt of reclaimed marshland that stretches from Shoeburyness to the Blackwater Estuary and includes Foulness, the largest island in the Thames Estuary; its lonely territory playing host, during the winter months, to an estimated 10,000 Brent Geese after they have flown south from their Arctic breeding grounds. The mudflats and winding creeks, with which this part of the coast abounds, has provided ideal conditions for the oysters that are produced here, and the ancient city of Colchester, the heart of the trade, traditionally holds an annual oyster feast that is quite unique.

For most people it would be impossible to divorce the Suffolk that we see today from the county that John Constable painted and which was his home. He was born in the village of East Bergholt and spent much of his life painting the countryside he knew and loved. The River Stour and its locks and banks were especial favourites with him and formed the subjects of many of his best-loved works. Possibly the best known, and certainly the one most visited by tourists, is Willy Lott's Cottage at Flatford Mill. Carefully preserved, it remains almost unchanged to this day and looks very much as it must have done to the artist when he sat down by the water with his canvas and brushes.

Norfolk is synonymous with 'The Broads', some 200 miles of open expanse of water with navigable approach channels which, linked with lakes, rivers and waterways – some man made – make up this delightful area that is seen to advantage from one of the many boats on hire to tourists. Because of the flat, open landscape in this part of the country, wind-driven mills were for many years used to grind corn, and it is estimated that there were about one thousand five hundred such mills at work until a century ago. Although their numbers have dwindled since then, enough remain still to form a picturesque part of the rural landscape. The magnificent cathedral of Holy Trinity in Norwich is the only remaining example in England that conforms to the Apsidal plan, with the Bishop's throne behind the altar, a relic of the days in the early history of Christianity when Roman basilicas were used in the practise of the new religion. While Norwich undoubtedly exhibits a wealth of historic interest, its outskirts too have their charms: Caistor St Edmund, for example, four miles south of the cathedral city, so legend asserts, once formed part of Boadicea's capital.

Hereward the Wake is a legendary figure in English history. A Saxon noble at the time of the occupation of England by William the Conqueror, he resolved to continue the fight against the Normans, and was successful in this for a considerable time – greatly aided by the fact that he took refuge, with his followers, in the Fen country, on the Isle of Ely. The area was almost inaccessible, consisting largely of treacherous marshes, and it is doubtful if any army could ever have reached him, had he not been betrayed by the monks. Throughout the centuries that followed, work was carried out on the draining of the Fens, but it was not until the 18th century that the Isle of Ely ceased to be an island. Dominating those vast, hedgeless fields is the mediaeval triumph of Ely Cathedral, its unique and magnificent octagonal lantern one of the finest engineering feats of the Middle Ages.

Gentle, undulating hills and peaceful valleys give Cambridgeshire a feeling of space and tranquillity which also permeates its lovely university city of Cambridge. It is a city that requires time spent in exploration to appreciate fully its rare beauty and fascination. The Bridge of Sighs, built in the style of the famous bridge of the same name in Venice, seems not at all out of place in this very English of cities, where punts, instead of gondolas, glide peacefully along the waters of the river that it spans. Renowned colleges, charming churches, quaint little bookshops, and the broad, sweeping lawns of the Backs are among the many delights that the city has to offer. Perhaps of all the county's most famous literary figures, the name of Rupert Brooke first springs to mind. His poignant *War Sonnets* earned him fame and popularity during the First World War, and it was to his home in the 'Old Vicarage' at Grantchester, where the poet first lived after leaving King's College, that Brooke dedicated his nostalgic poem, composed in 1912, in a café in Berlin, which epitomises the heartache experienced by many English exiles, particularly during periods of war.

Gloucestershire is inevitably linked with the Cotswold Hills that dominate its eastern half, while the mighty Severn River in the west effectively cut the county into two parts for many years, until the opening of the magnificent suspension bridge, in 1966, gave access to the verdant Forest of Dean, clothed with the delicious green mantle of an estimated 20 million trees. At the heart of the Severn Valley lies Gloucester, a rich agricultural centre in Roman times: its majestic cathedral containing the second largest mediaeval stained-glass window in the country.

To the west of the Malvern Hills and the lush orchards and market gardens of Worcestershire's Vale of Evesham, lies richly-wooded Herefordshire, famed for its apples (accounting for over half of the country's cider production) as well as the white-faced breed of cattle which have been used all over the world to improve other breeds; its historic cathedral city, once the Saxon capital of West Mercia, straddling the meandering Wye River. Even before the Norman conquest Herefordshire, a prime target on the Welsh border, was defended by stout castles against raiders from the Black Mountains which flank the west of the county, and on scenic Symonds Yat can be seen the remains of one of those strongholds, that of Goodrich Castle, which eventually fell to the troops of Oliver Cromwell during the Civil War.

It is hard to believe that the sprawling and highly industrialised conurbation of Birmingham – Britain's second largest city with a population well in excess of one million – at the heart of the Midland plain was, in Shakespeare's day, a thriving market town surrounded by open fields, with the Forest of Arden, north and west of the Avon River, covering some 200 square miles with leafy greenery. Yet not far from the city a wealth of picturesque villages and historic houses nestle amid the undulating countryside. Between Birmingham and Coventry, an important city since the 14th century, and famed for its controversial cathedral that was designed by Sir Basil Spence and consecrated in 1962, as well as its mediaeval 'streaker' Lady Godiva (the wife of Leofric, Earl of Mercia) who is reputed to have ridden naked through its streets in protest at the oppression of its inhabitants, stands the village of Meriden with its famous cross. Here too, is Packwood House with its remarkable 17th-century garden of shaped yew trees symbolising the Sermon on the Mount, and Compton Wynyates, one of the most beautiful Tudor houses in England, and the site of the first major battle of the Civil War, in 1642, at high-ridged Edge Hill. South of Coventry the mediaeval fortress of Warwick Castle dominates the wide Avon as it flows gently through the pastoral landscape that has changed little since Warwickshire's famous bard inhabited the old market town of Stratford-upon-Avon. This famous birthplace of William Shakespeare, with its half-timbered black and white houses and red-brick Royal Shakespeare Theatre, has become one of the world's most famous tourist attractions, and from the poet's birthplace, the early-16th-century building in Henley Street, to his tomb in Holy Trinity Church, the fascination of the beautiful old town and its close affinities with its son of genius can never fail to beguile and enrich each visitor.

Drained to the Wash by the Welland and the Nene rivers, the fertile soil of the famous foxhunting county of Northamptonshire patterns the northern section of its agricultural landscape with a quilting of rich, arable fields. Its bustling county town on the Nene has long been noted for its shoe industry – confirmed by the fact that it was responsible for the supply of some 1,500 shoes for Cromwell's Roundheads during the Civil War. Charles II, however, was less than pleased with Northampton's compliance to fill the order, and wreaked his revenge in the destruction of its castle and town walls.

Like its neighbouring county, Leicestershire is primarily agricultural, with the emphasis on dairy farming: the delicious blue-veined Stilton cheese being produced near Melton Mowbray, the world-famous home of pork pies and the Quorn Hunt. It was here on the county's productive plains, at Bosworth Field, that the long-fought duels of the Wars of the Roses finally came to an end, when Henry of Lancaster was proclaimed Henry VII on the death of his adversary, the ill-fated Richard III, of the House of York. At the hub of the county town of Leicester, which boasts a modern university and a history dating back over 2,000 years, rises a Victorian, Gothic-inspired clock tower that pays tribute to four of the city's notable benefactors. The most famous of these was the powerful baron, Simon de Montfort, Earl of Leicester, whose rebellion against the tyranny of his brother-in-law, Henry III, led, in 1265, to the establishment of the first English Parliament.

South of the Severn River, the rich, sheep-farming country on the edge of the Clun Forest, dominated by the limestone ridge of Wenlock Edge, which was immortalised by A.E. Housman in *A Shropshire Lad*, is contrasted with the wild heathlands and windswept moors that mark the Welsh border, in Salop's fascinating southwest corner. Here stand the relics of fortified strongholds that were built to defend against Celtic marauders – one of the most romantic being the abandoned, 11th-century sandstone castle of Ludlow, its crenellated towers perched high above the tranquil Teme River – as well as a wealth of well-preserved manor houses and clustered villages sporting their distinctive black and white, box-framed houses. North of the Long Mynd, a ten-mile stretch of bleak hills that crest a vast acreage of heath and moorland that is peppered by prehistoric defence earthworks and barrows, sits beautiful Shrewsbury, the county town, idyllically situated in a loop of the Severn. The surrounding countryside is punctuated by patches of hill country that includes the dramatic rock mass of the Wrekin, where a beacon once burned in warning of the approach of the Spanish Armada. During the 18th century Salop became the greatest iron-producing area in England; the town of Ironbridge, perched on the slopes of the steep and narrow gorge swept by the Severn River, gaining fame when Abraham Darby constructed the world's first cast-iron bridge, in 1779. Today the 200-ft bridge, cast in the designer's foundry at Coalbrookdale, is restricted to pedestrians.

Fine glazed china decorated with a spectrum of rainbow colours and gaily-patterned earthenware; exquisitely moulded figurines and exotic vases; these are just some of the wares of 'The Potteries', the north Staffordshire region that has become famous throughout the world for its handsome artifacts and which is inextricably linked with the most noted porcelain and pottery manufacturing names of Wedgwood, Spode, Copeland and Minton. Centred around Stoke-on-Trent, the city was formed in the early part of the 20th century by the amalgamation of the five towns of Burslem, Hanley, Longton, Stoke and Tunstall, which featured prominently in the memorable novels of Arnold Bennett, and a sixth town, Fenton. It was over two centuries ago that Josiah Wedgwood brought lasting fame to the area, aided by the creative genius of his designer John Flaxman, although the industry is known to have existed long before the Roman occupation. Away from the busy areas of commerce, however, Staffordshire has its great share of natural beauty, one of the most outstanding features being glorious Cannock Chase, an oasis of heath and forest land that once formed a vast hunting ground for Plantagenet kings, which lies on the verge of south Staffordshire's Black Country.

Derbyshire's Peak District, with its lush valleys and cascading streams, winding rivers and tree-studded hills, great rocky crags and gentle undulating pastures, has been compared to the countryside of Switzerland, and has a scenic splendour that would be difficult to surpass anywhere in the world. It came as no surprise, therefore, when in 1951 over five hundred square miles of the county were designated an area of outstanding beauty and became Britain's first National Park. As might be expected in such a lovely setting, great country houses were built here by famous families. South of the town of Bakewell, famed as the home of the delicious Bakewell tarts, lies the turreted, mediaeval outline of Haddon Hall, a romantic old house surrounded by terraced gardens. Not far away, and in contrast to its almost rambling beauty, stands one of the truly great stately homes of England, the majestic, classical mansion of Chatsworth House, set amid exquisite landscaped grounds, and built for the first Duke of Devonshire in the early 18th century.

While part of Nottinghamshire's face undeniably reveals the scars of industrialisation, notably in the collieries and their attendant slag heaps across the northwest coalfield belt, so vividly portrayed in the works of D.H. Lawrence, its boundaries encompass not only 200,000 acres of flat agricultural land of the Isle of Axholme, which was drained by the Dutchman, Cornelius Vermuyden in the 17th century, but also the green woodlands of romantic Sherwood Forest, the home of England's most popular folk hero, the elusive Robin Hood. It is true that the famous outlaw is identified with no less than ten other counties in the country and that Barnsdale Forest in Yorkshire has an equal claim to be called his home, yet somehow the remnants of the once-vast Sherwood Forest seem richer in association with the man whom tradition asserts is more fact than fiction.

The ferry from Hull in Humberside makes its way across the River Humber to New Holland in Lincolnshire. The area has more in common with the low-lying country of Holland than just a name, for it too is just about at sea-level, and in springtime the fields are alive with the colours of the tulips that are grown in the rich soil of this part of the country. Yet not all the lands of Lincolnshire are flat and low-lying, by any means. There are also the rolling uplands of the Wolds, thick with sheep grazing on the pastures, and abundant in the wheat for which the area is so famous. In this countryside of hills and valleys may be found many charming villages and towns, including the birthplace of Alfred, Lord Tennyson, in Somersby. Of the county's many churches, abbeys, stately homes and other fine buildings, two stand out in particular, though for different reasons. The first is in the ancient town of Boston, on the River Witham and is known by the peculiar name of 'The Boston Stump'. It is, in fact, the tower of St Botolph's Church and is a landmark for many miles. The second is, not surprisingly, the magnificent cathedral that dominates the city of Lincoln and which contains, in the Angel Choir, the finest Decorated work to be found in the country.

Grassy banks of yellow-headed buttercups; wooded hilltops bearing traces of long-ago Roman occupation; gentle rivers curving through fertile farmland; picturesque towns with their distinctive 'magpie' houses, and timbered manors, beautifully illustrated in the 15th-century building of Bramall Hall and 16th-century Little Moreton Hall, are part of the immense, individual charm of Cheshire. It was at Knutsford that Mrs Gaskell drew inspiration for her charming novel, *Cranford*, although the sight of the giant radio telescope of Jodrell Bank, standing like some science fiction creation six miles south of the town, would doubtfully have gained the approbation of her 'genteel' ladies, to whom satellites, radio signals and far-distant galaxies would have been an undreamed-of horror! Chester, the county town, skirted by the meandering River Dee, is an ancient, walled city of Roman origin, with a wealth of historic interest. Probably its most famous feature is The Rows, which consists of galleried streets of shops, reached by stairways; a feature that is quite unique.

Between the estuaries of the Rivers Mersey and Dee lies the

Wirral Peninsula, the heart of the Merseyside playground, where miles of sand-dune-edged beaches are connected to the industrialised hub of Birkenhead by wharves and docks. Joined to this important flour-milling and shipbuilding centre by two tunnels under the Mersey, is the 13th-century fishing village that grew phenomenally during the Industrial Revolution: Liverpool. From the seven-mile stretch of densely-packed dockland along its waterfront rises the idiosyncratic outline of the celebrated Liver Building, its two main towers topped by mythical 'Liver' birds, after which the city is said to have been named. This cosmopolitan city also boasts two cathedrals, each of distinct, ecclesiastical architecture: Sir Giles Gilbert Scott's Gothic-inspired Anglican Cathedral and Sir Frederick Gibberd's contemporary Roman Catholic Metropolitan Cathedral, with its huge, conical 'lantern'.

Until the reorganisation of the county boundaries in 1974, Manchester, built by Agricola's legions on the banks of the Irwell River, was the mighty commercial hub of Lancashire, a 14th-century county palatine, bordered by the wild Pennine Moors on its eastern flank and by fertile lowlands to the west, against the Irish Sea. It is along this coastline, a popular resort area since the mid-18th century, that is sited the North West's busiest and most famous holiday centre of Blackpool, dominated by its 518-ft tower that oversees the six-mile-long promenade, noted for its spectacular autumn illuminations. Offshore lies one of the smallest independent sovereign countries under the Crown, the tiny Isle of Man, its picturesque scenery and exceptionally mild climate providing ideal conditions for holiday activities. Douglas, the island's capital, is the home of the Tynwald, the Manx Parliament with Scandinavian origins that are earlier than those of Westminster.

Harnessed to the vast conurbation of Greater Manchester, and its fan of industrial centres that include the major cotton-spinning towns of Bolton and Oldham, Manchester's importance as a key cotton centre was firmly rooted during the 18th century, although Flemish weavers had established the weaving tradition over four hundred years earlier. This inland city became one of the country's largest seaports, handling the export of raw cotton and importing finished textiles, with the construction of the 35-mile-long Manchester Ship Canal, which was opened in 1894. Although ravaged by the effects of the Industrial Revolution and by bomb damage during the Second World War, the city's extensive redevelopment schemes have already greatly altered and enhanced its visual image, but its crowning glory, however, is still the magnificent 15th-century Perpendicular Gothic Cathedral, its soaring, 280-ft tower containing a carillon of 23 bells.

Lake-strewn valleys amid craggy mountains, fern-covered hillsides and forested woodlands, tumbling waterfalls and carpets of wild flowers; little wonder that the spectacular scenery of Cumbria's Lake District inspired the celebrated 'Lake Poets' – Wordsworth, Southey and Coleridge – and a host of writers such as Beatrix Potter, who wrote and illustrated some of her charming children's books at Hill Top Farm in the village of Sawrey. Painters and photographers, sportsmen and ramblers, and, of course, mountaineers, who challenge the forbidding massifs that include Skiddaw, Helvellyn and England's second highest peak, Scafell, have also long been attracted to the Lakeland region, where, it is claimed, the sport of rock-climbing originated. The two largest lakes, Ullswater and Windermere, are set amid a landscape that has remained virtually unchanged since Wordsworth first saw his 'host of golden daffodils', while the Tarns, near Coniston, is considered by many to be the prettiest of all the area's lakes. Yet Cumbria does not consist solely of Lakeland, as unquestionable as its beauty is. The Border region beyond Carlisle is rich in historical associations and remains. Here stand the fragments of the northern limit of the Roman Empire – Hadrian's Wall – and a wealth of prehistoric sites and castles, like the Border fortress of Carlisle Castle.

Centred around the Humber Estuary, the county of Humberside comprises most of the old East Riding of Yorkshire plus the area around Goole. It was along the chalk-cliffed coastline where the Yorkshire Wolds terminate in the rocky promontory of Flamborough Head, just beyond the popular seaside resort of Bridlington, that the Vikings successfully swept ashore in the 10th century – their once-victorious cries now echoed by the high-pitched shrieks of thousands of seabirds which today inhabit the striking northern cliffs. Officially Kingston-upon-Hull, Hull, lying on the broad Humber River and one of the country's leading seaports, is renowned for its great fishing fleets which have justly earned their reputation of landing a greater quantity of fish than any other British port. The city is also remembered as the native town of the dedicated anti-slavery campaigner William Wilberforce, whose home is now a museum.

Formed mainly from the former North Riding, the diverse landscape of North Yorkshire, littered with the marks of man from time immemorial, encompasses the wild, bleak North York Moors that rise beyond the Vale of Pickering, bordering the Yorkshire Wolds, and the broad expanse of the fertile Vale of York which is flanked to the west by the spectacular scenery of the Yorkshire Dales as they merge with England's spiny backbone, the Pennine Chain. In a region crammed with so many historical relics, it is difficult to do other than just pluck at random some of its bright jewels: close to Malton stands one of England's most palatial mansions in a perfectly matched setting, that of Castle Howard, created for the 3rd Earl of Carlisle by Sir John Vanbrugh between 1699 and 1726; by the Wharfe River tower stand the splendid ruined remains of twelfth-century Bolton Abbey, and near Helmsley, above the River Rye, is sited one of the country's earliest Cistercian houses, magnificent Rievaulx Abbey, its ruined splendour seen to perfection against the densely-wooded backdrop. Popular seaside resorts, such as Scarborough and Whitby, dot its coastline; dignified towns, like the fashionable inland spa of Harrogate, which is also a noted conference centre, add to its lustre, whilst a host of picturesque villages are scattered across its length and breadth. As if this were not enough, proud Yorkshiremen can also boast of their ancient Roman garrison-town of Eboracum – glorious York – much of its 2,000 years of history still vividly tangible inside the city walls. Its present name is derived from Jorvik, so-called by the invading Danes who captured the city during the 9th century. Of all its treasures, however, pride of place must go to its breathtaking Minster, 'a poem of stone' that took over two and a half centuries to complete, between 1220 and 1470.

Famed for its woollen industry, centred on the important trading communities that include Bradford, Leeds and Halifax, which grew phenomenally during the Industrial Revolution as the old cottage industries moved closer to the coalfields and their valuable source of fuel, the West Yorkshire Moors, penetrated by the Aire and Calder rivers, have long supported the white-fleeced sheep that have grazed on the moorland for centuries past. It was this same bleak moorland turf that was trod by the famous Brontë family – Emily, Charlotte, Anne and Branwell, who lived in the Old Parsonage at Haworth, a square, sandstone house that has been the Bronte" Museum since 1928.

Below the moors the industrial heart of Yorkshire is contained within the metropolitan county of South Yorkshire. This largely industrialised region, especially in the Don Valley, is renowned for its iron and steel manufacture. Sheffield, set in an amphitheatre of the South Pennine slopes, is synonymous with the steel and cutlery industry, for the city has produced knife blades for almost seven centuries.

Rugged and tempered like the stalwart people who laid not only their endeavour but also their landscape at the feet of progress during the Industrial Revolution, the counties of Cleveland, Durham and Tyne & Wear still bear, inevitably, the symbols that mark the region's industrial greatness. Yet it would be erroneous to suppose that the counties consist solely of the features of shipbuilding, iron, steel and chemical industries, for they too have their share of beauty, and nowhere is this more apparent than in the splendid cathedral city of Durham, built in a loop of the River Wear; its magnificent Norman Cathedral a shrine of St Cuthbert and also containing the tomb of the Venerable Bede within its richly ornamented interior. Along the coastline picturesque resorts boast long stretches of sandy beaches, while some of the finest scenery of the Pennine Chain is evident on the west Durham Moors.

Rich in history, England's most northerly county of Northumberland, bounded on the north by Scotland across the River Tweed and the Cheviot Hills, and flanked to the east by the

North Sea, contains one of the most famous of all Roman remains – the spectacular relic of Hadrian's Wall which slices across the county from Haltwhistle to Wallsend in Tyne & Wear. Today, the tranquil farmland, south of the River Tweed, belies the savagery of the fierce border clashes – vividly evoked by the area's many ancient fortresses – perhaps the bloodiest that of Flodden Field where, in 1513, the blood of James IV and thousands of Scots and Englishmen was spilled on the earth now covered by tall ears of corn that flutter in the breeze. At Berwick-upon-Tweed, England's northernmost town, which was once a great Scottish port, stands an impressive bridge of 17th-century origin, with no less than 15 arches; built by order of James I to connect the town of Tweedmouth on the opposite side of the estuary.

In any book on a country, however wide the coverage or strong the intent, a vast amount is inevitably omitted. It would be foolish to suppose that these pages only record the best that is to be seen and that there is little else worth showing. At best a book such as this can only serve to awaken an interest in objects and places that the reader may not be aware of, or to tinge with nostalgia that with which the reader is familiar, and in so doing to present just a few of the riches with which this country is so liberally endowed.

Fields near the village of Shere, Surrey.

Above: the waters of High Force, in Gowbarrow Park near Ullswater, and (facing page) quiet southern farmland at Harcombe. Overleaf: Potter Heigham (left) provides attractive moorings for yachts on the Norfolk Broads. (Right) a less populated waterway flows through Lower Slaughter in Gloucestershire.

These pages: sunrise over the farmland of Surrey, and (overleaf, left) poppies border a Suffolk wheatfield. Overleaf: (right) where the South Downs meet the sea between Beachy Head and the mouth of the Cuckmore River the cliffs are broken by the dramatic cleft of Birling Gap.

Above: the narrow gorge of Symond's Yat in Hereford and Worcester. Right: Cambridge University buildings, with the chapel of King's College at their centre. Overleaf: (left) the Weavers, overlooking the River Stour in Canterbury. (Right) the harbour at Newquay, Cornwall.

Winter mountains and farmland: the splendour of Helvellyn and Thirlmere (above, far left), the beauty and isolation of Haweswater (left) and the Crinkle Crags and Blowfell (far left). Overleaf: (left) the Severn Bridge connects Aust and Beachley, and carries the M4 motorway into Wales. (Right) evening view over Whitby's fishing harbour, from the steps leading to Whitby Abbey.

Above: autumn at Parham Park in West Sussex, and (facing page) the fifteenth century manor of Athelhampton House in Dorset, mirrored in its still pool. Overleaf: Sir Edward Dalyngrigge was granted a special licence by the Crown to build Bodiam Castle (left), in 1385, to protect his estate from incursions by the French. (Right) Beaulieu Abbey, on the estuary of the Beaulieu River in Hampshire.

Above: cows graze on rich farmland at Harringworth in Northamptonshire, and (facing page) a 'green lane' winds its way across upland pastures on the North Yorkshire Moors. Overleaf: the spectacular rock formations of the Dorset coast include (left) the arch of Durdle Door, and (right) Old Harry Rocks at Studland Bay.

(Above) the Severn Estuary, spanned by the Severn Bridge. Facing page: the prehistoric, megalithic stone circle of Stonehenge, on Salisbury Plain, Wiltshire. Overleaf: the small harbour of Boscastle in Cornwall (left) is sheltered by colourful cliffs on either side. (Right) Oakwood Hill church in Surrey.

Left: bracken-covered slopes surround Rydal Water and Grasmere, and (above) the Langdale Pikes rise to snowy peaks in the Lake District. (Top) the ruins of a milecastle punctuate the 73-mile-long barrier of Hadrian's Wall.
Overleaf: (left) mellow stone cottages in the Gloucestershire village of Bilbury. (Right) the ruins of twelfth century Rievaulx Abbey in Ryedale, Yorkshire. This Cistercian monastery was the centre of the great Christianising mission of St Bernard of Clairvaux to the north of England.

Above: wintry Troutbeck Park in Cumbria. Facing page: the granite mass of Land's End, the westernmost point on the mainland of England, lies at the end of the Penwith Peninsula in Cornwall. Overleaf: (left) spring daffodils in Richmond Park and (right) summer amongst the whitewashed cottages of Bickleigh on the River Exe, Devon.

Above: St Mary's church, in the town of Warwick, contains the beautiful fifteenth century Beauchamp Chapel.
Facing page: the village green at Finchingfield in Essex. Overleaf: patchwork fields surround the village
of Hurstbourne Tarrant, Hampshire, and (right) summer cottages at Welford-on-Avon in Warwickshire.

The fifteenth century tower of St Mary's church rises above the village of Cerne Abbas in Dorset
(above). Facing page: the South Downs near Lewes in Sussex. Overleaf: (right) well-preserved
Houghton Mill in Cambridgeshire, and (left) a water-mill in Hambleden, Buckinghamshire.

Above: autumn colours Symond's Yat, on a narrow loop of the River Wye in Hereford and Worcester. Right: the medieval splendour of Canterbury Cathedral, which was begun in 1070 by Lanfranc, the city's first Norman archbishop. Overleaf: (left) old water-mill on the River Darent in Farningham, Kent, and (right) the Rothay beck at Ambleside.

63

Above: the chalk cliffs of the Isle of Purbeck, Dorset, and (facing page) the harbour and single, steep street of Clovelly in Devon. Overleaf: (left) autumn at Burnham Beeches in Buckinghamshire. (Right) magnificent gardens, originally laid out by Henry Hoare, surround the eighteenth century mansion of Stourhead in Wiltshire.

Facing page: seventeenth century market hall in the Cotswold town of Chipping Camden, Gloucestershire. Above: the Jacobean facade of Blickling Hall in Norfolk. The estate was once owned by the Boleyn family; it is said that Anne Boleyn was born and spent her childhood in an earlier house on the site. Overleaf: (left) Sandringham House in Norfolk, and (right) Finchingfield, Essex.

Above: the harbour at Ilfracombe in Devon, and (facing page) the river at Henley-on-Thames in Oxfordshire, where the famous regatta is held annually in the first week of July. Overleaf: (left) Worcester Cathedral was founded in 680, though the present building is of Norman through to the fourteenth century date. (Right) summer gardens at West Dean in Sussex.

74

Above: fields of clover and buttercups in the Yorkshire Dales, and (facing page) bluebells.
Overleaf: (left) sixteenth century cottages on the banks of the Stour, in Canterbury, and
(right) half-timbered houses in Water Street, in the old wool town of Lavenham, Suffolk.

Left: Towan Head stretches for nearly a mile out to sea at Newquay in Cornwall, and (top) rocky headlands near Land's End. Above: Devon thatch, on the River Exe at Bickleigh. Overleaf: (left) the cottage where Thomas Hardy was born, in 1840, is carefully preserved in the Dorset village of Higher Bockhampton. (Right) the yellow stone of Hidcote Manor in Gloucestershire.

Above: the village of Swan Green in Dorset. Facing page: view over the spa town of Matlock Bath in Derbyshire.
Overleaf: (left) Bodiam Castle, in East Sussex, was restored by Lord Curzon in 1925. (Right) west of
Eastbourne, the coastline is dominated by chalk cliffs rising 600 feet above sea level at Beachy Head.

Above: Aira Force near Ullswater in the Lake District. Facing page: the square tower of Combe Martin church in Devon. Overleaf: (left) Bamburgh Castle in Northumberland was founded in the sixth century by Ida, king of the Anglo-Saxon kingdom of Bernicia, and rebuilt after the Norman conquest. (Right) Hadrian's Wall, contructed by the Romans to secure their northern British border.

Facing page: mellow Gloucestershire stone cottages, Naunton, and (above) a Yorkshire farm at Bransdale. Overleaf: (left) Kingswear, seen from Dartmouth across the River Dart, and (right) red sands at the resort of Teignmouth, Devon.

Facing page: Durham Cathedral, built on a high rock and surrounded on three sides by the River Wear, was begun in 1093 by Bishop William of Calais. Above: dawn over Corfe Castle in Dorset. Overleaf: (left) the Cotswold village of Broadway, and (right) Little Snoring church in the flat farmland of Norfolk.

Facing page: steep bay at Treen in Cornwall, and (above) the earthworks at Castle Rising in Norfolk, upon which the Norman motte and bailey castle was superimposed. Overleaf: (left) Florentine, shop-lined Pulteney Bridge in Bath, designed by the eighteenth century architect Robert Adam. (Right) Bainbridge in Wensleydale, Yorkshire.

Above: Cumbrian autumn. Top: the waterfall of High
Force flows down into Ullswater (top, far right)
in the Lake District. Right: the quiet splendour
of Derwentwater, and (bottom, far right) the snow
covered Langdale Pikes contrast with the flat
landscape of Norfolk (centre, far right).
Overleaf: (left) the lovely Tudor house of Compton
Wynyates in Warickshire. (Right) Wells Cathedral
seen from the gardens of the Bishops Palace,
Somerset.

107

Facing page: the half-timbered farmhouse at Winkworth Farm in Hascombe, Surrey. Above: the church of St Andrew's at Naunton, Gloucestershire. Overleaf: (left) Crummock Water in the Lake District. (Right) pleasure boats on the Thames, seen from Richmond Hill.

The outer ring of sarsen stones surrounding Avebury stone circle (above) measures 1,350 ft in diameter, and encircles the whole village. Facing page: the birthplace of Anne Hathaway, wife of William Shakespeare, in Shottery, Warwickshire. Overleaf: (left) the great limestone arch of Durdle Door, and (right) sheltered Man o'War Bay, on the Isle of Purbeck, Dorset.

Facing page: limestone walls enclose rough hill pasture in the Yorkshire dales at Malham, and (above) the richer fields of the valley floor. Overleaf: (left) the Tudor manor house of Sissinghurst Castle, set in fine gardens. (Right) Leeds Castle, a twelfth century stronghold with later additions, is built on two islands in a lake formed by the damming of the River Len in Kent.

Above: busy harbour at Yarmouth on the Isle of Wight. Facing page: the Dorset resort of Swanage on the Isle of Purbeck, viewed from sheltering Ballad Down. Overleaf: sunrise and snow colour the Surrey countryside.

Above: Windsor Castle and swans on the River Thames, Berkshire. Facing page: the restored fourteenth century church at Earls Colne in Essex. Overleaf: (left) mist on Bowness in the Lake District. (Right) the Isabella Plantation in Richmond Park.

126

Facing page: the Cathedral dominates the town of Canterbury. Above: spring sunshine. Overleaf: (left) summer in the grounds of Christ Church College, Oxford, founded by Cardinal Wolsey in 1525. (Right) peaceful Ullswater in the Lake District.

Above: York's medieval city walls, which still extend for three miles, incorporate four fine gates, and York Minster. Facing page: Pulteney Bridge in Bath, designed by Robert Adam to reflect the Ponte Vecchio in Florence. Overleaf: (left) the fishing village of Polperro, Cornwall. (Right) Cheddar Gorge in Somerset.

Above: Mothecombe Bay in South Devon. Facing page: dawn mist over the Surrey landscape.
Overleaf: (left) the village of Sonning, where an eleven-arch bridge spans the Thames, and
(right) the Elizabethan manor of Mapledurham House, beside the Thames in Oxfordshire.

The old ford at the centre of Kersey in Suffolk (above). William Shakespeare married Anne Hathaway, born at Shottery (facing page), at eighteen, and she bore him a daughter and twins, Hamnet and Judith. Overleaf: (left) Sutton Place in Surrey. (Right) the resort of Eastbourne on the south coast, created by the Duke of Devonshire in the nineteenth century to rival Brighton.

Facing page: the University of Oxford, where the distinctive, circular Radcliffe Camera stands before the great quad of All Soul's College, with those of New College and Queens College beyond. Top: hot canal day at Tiverton, Devon, and (above) a Surrey lakeside. Overleaf: (left) Ross-on-Wye lies within a bend of the river, and (right) Aylesford stands reflected in the Medway, Kent.

Bracken covered slopes above Ladybower Reservoir in the Peak District (above), and Elter
Water in Cumbria (facing page). Overleaf: (left) steep, cobbled Gold Hill in Shaftesbury
overlooks misty Dorset farmland. (Right) Whitchurch on the River Thames in Oxfordshire.

Above: the moated manor house of Hever Castle, Kent, dates from the thirteenth century. Anne Boleyn spent her girlhood here, and Henry VIII was a frequent visitor. When the Astor family bought the house in 1903 they took up the Tudor theme, building a 'village' of Tudor-style houses across the moat. Facing page: church at Medmenham in Buckinghamshire. Overleaf: (left) Goring lock on the River Thames. (Right) the fishing harbour at Whitby in Yorkshire.

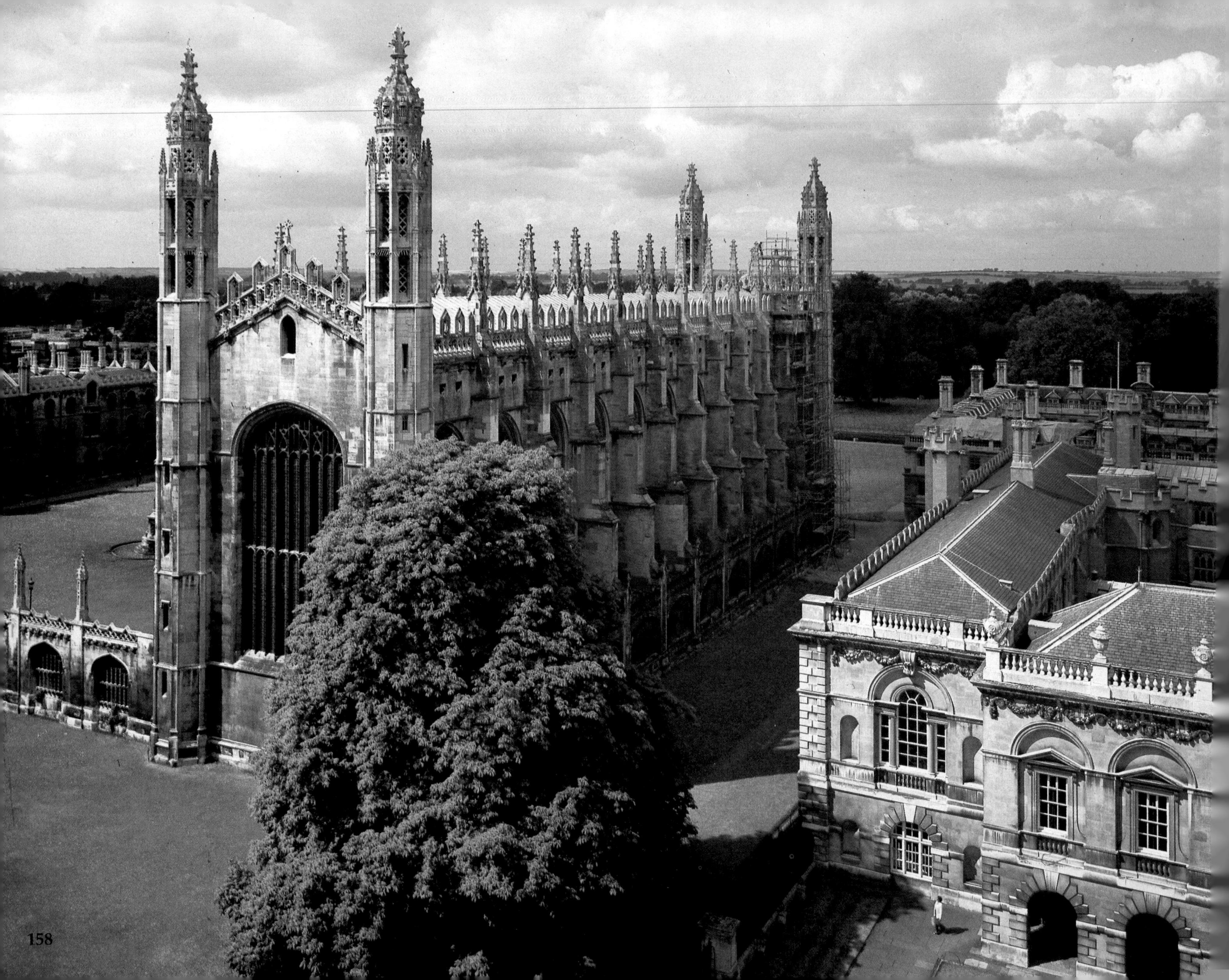

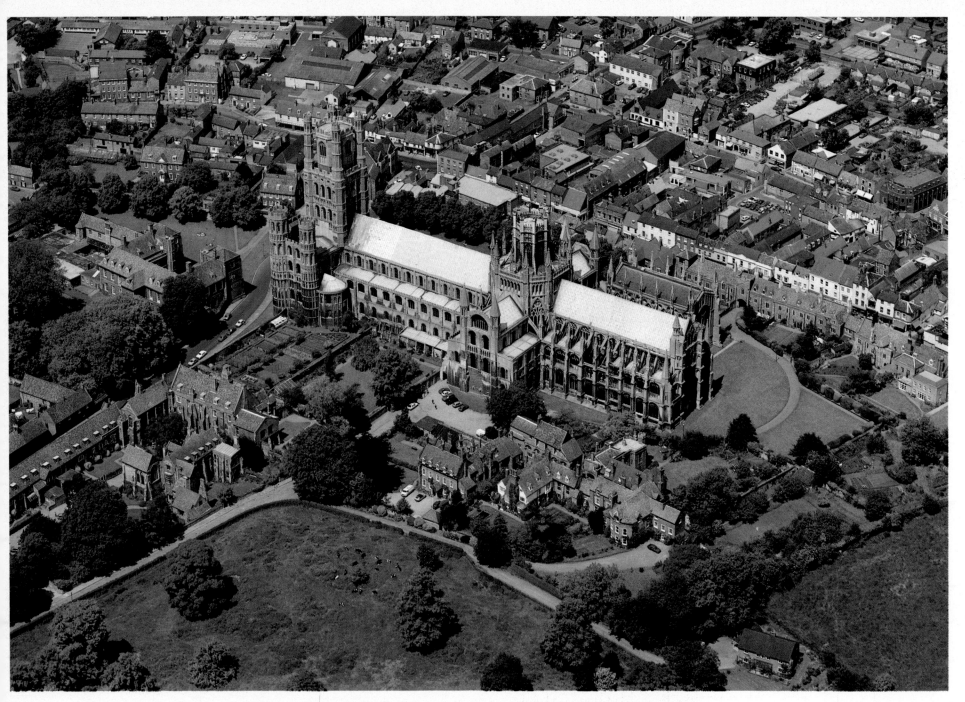

Facing page: King's College Chapel, Cambridge, was begun by Henry VI in 1446, interrupted by the War of the Roses, and completed in 1515. Flemish craftsmen spent the following twenty-six years putting in the brilliantly coloured stained glass. Above: eleventh century Ely Cathedral, with its distinctive octagonal lantern tower, Cambridgeshire.

INDEX